The Quick Wise Guide to Fundraising Readiness

HOW TO PREPARE YOUR
NONPROFIT TO RAISE FUNDS

Waddy Thompson

Stitch-in-Time Books

© 2018 by Waddy Thompson

All rights reserved. No part of this book shall be reproduced, stored in a retrieval system, or transmitted by any means, electronic, mechanical, photocopying, recording, or otherwise, without written permission from the publisher. No patent liability is assumed with respect to the use of the information contained herein. Although every precaution has been taken in the preparation of this book, the publisher and author assume no responsibility for errors or omissions. Neither is any liability assumed for damages resulting from the use of information contained herein.

Note: This publication contains the opinions and ideas of its author. It is intended to provide helpful and informative material on the subject matter covered. It is sold with the understanding that the author and publisher are not engaged in rendering professional services in it. If the reader requires personal assistance or advice, a competent professional should be consulted.

The author specifically disclaims any responsibility for any liability, loss, or risk, personal or otherwise, that is incurred as a consequence, directly or indirectly, of the use and application of any of the contents of this book.

The *Quick* Wise Guide to Fundraising Readiness
Waddy Thompson
First edition January 2018
Stitch-in-Time Books, Sarasota, Florida, USA

ISBN: 978-0-9985124-5-7

www.grantadviser.com

Cover concept by Flyleaf Creative; design by Jakob Vala
Copyediting by Georgette Beatty
Images used under license from Shutterstock.com
Author photo by Jan Lasalle

Contents

Introduction 1

Chapter 1: Human Resources 3

    Ideal Characteristics of a Fundraiser . 3

    Board Members 4

        Training Your Board 5

        Expanding Your Board 6

    Other Volunteers 7

    Staff and Consultants 7

        Your First Development Staff Member 9

Chapter 2: Data Management 10

Chapter 3: Supporting Materials 17

    Nonprofit Status 17

    Board List 18

    State and/or Federal 19

    Financial Reports 19

    Audited Financial Statements 19

    Budgets 20

    Staff Information 21

    Mission Statement 21

- History and Background 21
- Testimonials 22
- Case Statement 22
- Video 22
- Marketing Materials 23
- Client Demographics 23
- Public Information 24

Chapter 4: Soliciting Individuals 25
- Personal Solicitations 25
- Mail and Email Solicitations 26
- Crowdfunding 27
- Peer-to-Peer Fundraising 28
- Planned Giving 29

Chapter 5: Special Events 31

Chapter 6: Foundations 35

Chapter 7: Corporations 38
- Sponsorships 38
- In-Kind Support 39
- Grants 39

Chapter 8: Government Agencies 41

Glossary 43

Additional Resources 46
- Getting Started 46

Mission Statements 46
Budgets 47
Data Management 47
Individual Giving 47
Grant Writing Guides and Research .48
Corporate Fundraising 50
About the Author 51

Introduction

Imagine . . . Your nonprofit has a clear purpose and is doing great work. A few contributions have come in from friends of the founder and board members, but you need more income to carry out your programs in the manner and in the scale that you envision them.

It would be great to receive contributions from more people, and it would be really nice to get a few big checks from foundations—if only you could figure out how to fundraise.

Does that sound familiar? If so, read *The Quick Wise Guide to Fundraising Readiness* before you make any false starts or hire a fundraiser to help you. This book explains everything you need to know before you start asking anyone for a donation.

Step by step, I take you through the process that will bring your nonprofit to fundraising readiness, helping you put in place the people, infrastructure, and materials that will help your first moves in fundraising be successful ones.

In addition, I help you evaluate whether different types of fundraising (government grants, for example) will be likely sources of income.

To top it all off, you'll find at the back of the book a glossary of fundraising terms (that appear in italics in the text) and a list of resources that will help you further explore various aspects of fundraising.

Let's get ready to fundraise!

Foundation Grants **BOARDS** Individual Donors **CRM Software**
FUNDRAISING
Corporate Sponsorship
Special Events
Mission
Statements
Planned Giving

Chapter 1

Human Resources

Fundraising is all about people. We don't raise funds from corporations; we raise funds from people who work for corporations. Ditto for foundations and government agencies. Developing relationships is the most important part of fundraising, so it's important to start with the right kinds of people to do your fundraising. These include board members, volunteers, staff, and consultants.

Ideal Characteristics of a Fundraiser

Anyone who has done fundraising before is, of course, a valuable asset to your fundraising efforts, but just as importantly, you want to have people with the right characteristics working with you.

Someone with natural curiosity makes the best fundraiser. A curious person is interested in other people—where they come from, where they are going, what makes them tick—and can retain that information and use it to create personalized approaches. For example, someone with young children might be particularly interested in education; a person with business interests in China might have reason to support a show of Chinese art.

You also want someone who possesses a high level of enthusiasm for what you do. Genuine excitement about your program will be infectious and help convince others to support your work.

In addition, you want someone dedicated to your organization—who believes wholeheartedly in what you do. The best fundraisers can speak passionately about what your nonprofit means to them personally.

Board Members

If yours is a new nonprofit, people close to the founder and/or practitioners in the field will likely make up your board of directors. These people might or might not be accustomed to or comfortable with fundraising. You can train those already on the board to be fundraisers, or you can expand your board to include people who will help you fundraise. You'll probably want to do both.

Before you start to work on fundraising from your board, you need to decide if you will have a minimum giving requirement for board members. Nonprofits have mixed results establishing a hard-and-fast minimum gift. In some cases, the minimum becomes the *de facto* maximum gift. Some nonprofits ask that board members instead make a gift that is significant to them or one that at least equals any other charitable gift they make. Either rule provides a lot of leeway for hardworking practitioners to feel they are contributing fairly while making more affluent board members consider larger gifts in line with their other giving and their capacity to give.

Next, consider what you will count as a major gift that might be solicited personally by a board member. For many small nonprofits, the threshold is $1,000, but it might be more or less for your nonprofit. (And at the other extreme, I know of a major museum where people aren't considered major donors until they are giving $5 million annually!)

Training Your Board

There are a number of online guides about how to ask for donations (see the list of additional resources at the end of this book), and the right consultant (see below) can be of great help in training board members. I like to ask board members to start out by making thank-you phone calls. This task helps them get over the fear of making a blind call and of talking to a stranger about money; it also will have a tremendously positive effect on your donors. You can start with just a few board members making thank-you calls, and then you can have them report back to the full board on their experiences.

You also might create an opportunity for your board members to do some role play with each other, which should build confidence and help them feel more natural when asking for donations. Pairing a board member with a professional staff member or consultant to call on donors is usually very successful. In some cases, the board member might start the meeting by talking about what good work is being done, leaving the professional staff member to ask for the donation.

Expanding Your Board

In seeking new board members, first look for people capable of writing you a nice-sized check. Discuss with your current board members who among their contacts might be good board members as well as significant contributors. To expand beyond your board's contacts, you'll need to research people who are active in supporting similar organizations by using other groups' publicly available donor recognition lists. (Rarely does someone support only one nonprofit in an area that interests him.)

You also want people with connections and influence on your board. Investment bankers and lawyers who deal in trusts and estates frequently have extensive networks of clients and other professionals they can call on. Prominent business leaders in your community also will have great connections and can help your nonprofit become better known. But beware of the "over-boarded." I don't mean people who have fallen out of a boat, but rather people who already have several other board commitments. What is the chance that your organization will be their top priority if they've been raising money for two or three other nonprofits for years?

Some consultants and headhunters specialize in finding board members. Look to pay a flat fee for this service (not a percentage of what the new board member gives). You'll have to decide whether getting board members in this way is worth the expense.

Other Volunteers

Other kind and generous people might want to help you but are not in a position (time-wise or financially) to join your board. Welcome them with open arms! If they want to help you with fundraising, look for the same characteristics as you seek in board members. You likely will not have a specified minimum gift for volunteers, but no one should solicit funds for your nonprofit without first making their own gift, even if it's only five dollars. Their gifts are more about demonstrating a commitment to your nonprofit than they are about financial support. And it's actually easier to ask for a donation knowing that you have already done your part.

Staff and Consultants

When choosing an employee to work on fundraising, you want someone who has all of the characteristics enumerated earlier in this chapter and who is highly organized. There is no such thing as a successful yet disorganized fundraiser. Fundraising staff must track grant deadlines; coordinate the writing, printing, and mailing of appeal letters; remember which board members know which donors; and a million other details. Organizing information and sticking to schedules are essential skills for a fundraiser.

Although someone who has worked for a similar nonprofit will bring inside knowledge of your sector, remember that fundraising skills are completely transferable, and someone from a different type of nonprofit with more experience, greater curiosity, and better organizational skills might be preferable to a less experienced person from your field.

A fundraising consultant can help you jump-start your fundraising program. She will come with a wealth of knowledge about all the different aspects of fundraising and be able to help you prioritize your donor prospects. Try to find someone who works with small and/or start-up nonprofits. A consultant accustomed to working only with multimillion-dollar organizations with lots of support staff might have difficulty conceiving of a modest plan to get you started.

When it comes to paying a consultant, only hire someone who works for a flat fee. Taking a percentage of the money raised (rather than a flat fee) is contrary to the ethical standards of the Association of Fundraising Professionals, and it just makes sense. Many factors determine if someone makes a gift and how much he gives, ranging from his personal finances to the reputation of your nonprofit. Also, a consultant is a professional and deserves to make a reasonable fee even if your top five prospects give nothing.

Finally, beware of a consultant who promises to give you use of her donor list. Those names are probably supporters of her other clients; it's unethical for a fundraiser to share donors' personal information with another organization, and I don't think you will want her passing on your donor list to someone else at some point.

Your First Development Staff Member

Your first development staff member will likely need to be a jack-of-all-trades. No one will be expert in every area of fundraising, but here are some qualifications you will want to include in a job listing or description:

- Familiar with the use of donor software
- Knowledge of direct mail and email strategies
- Skilled writer able to create persuasive arguments for support
- Highly organized self-starter capable of working on several projects at once
- Excellent phone manner and comfortable working with all types of people

You might add that someone with grant or sponsorship experience is preferred and state a specific number of years of experience that is required—keeping in mind that the more years of experience, the higher the salary that will be expected.

Although you might give preference to someone who has previously worked in the same nonprofit sector (health, arts, social services, etc.), keep in mind that fundraising skills are completely transferable.

There are several online job listing services, but fundraisers are most likely to look at idealist.org, afpnet.org, and philanthropy.com. The first two do not charge fees to organizations posting a listing.

Chapter 2

Data Management

Whenever two or more fundraisers get together, eventually they end up talking about their fundraising software. Why? Because successful fundraising depends on data, including (1) knowing who has given what to your nonprofit, (2) people's specific interests and backgrounds, (3) their relationships with you (members, trustees, gala attendees, scholarship donors, etc.), and (4) their relationships with each other. In the process of developing your fundraising program, you will accumulate tons of information on your most important donors, and you must have the means to store and retrieve that information.

The best programs are correctly referred to as *constituent relationship management (CRM) systems* since they track the relationships of donors to the nonprofit and to each other, as well as the contributions they make and any other interactions you have with them. Many software programs are available to help you raise money. Some are only for capturing online donations whereas others help you with *peer-to-peer fundraising*, but you want to start out with a full-featured constituent management system, and it doesn't have to cost a fortune.

Fundraising programs live or die by the quality of their donor data. The more you know, the better you can engage donors and the more they will donate to your cause!

There are many data management programs out there at a staggering range of prices. Before I make my specific recommendations, here is what—at minimum—you want your database to be able to do:

1. Tracking current names and addresses is the most basic management tool. This might also include nicknames, summer/winter addresses, spouse names, and children's names and ages. Having one database for all of your organization's constituents is a time saver and money raiser, so don't have different databases for your clients, donors, press contacts, etc.

2. The next most important facility is tracking gifts, including what they were given for, what solicitation produced them, and how they were transmitted (check, credit card, direct transfer, stock transfer, etc.). It is also helpful if you can track who solicited the gift and credit that person with raising that money. This is known as creating a *soft credit* that appears in the solicitor's record, but the software totals it separately from the solicitor's own contributions. For example, board member Mary Smith gave $4,000 this year, plus gifts from the friends she solicited brought in $3,500. The database therefore shows that she was responsible for $7,500, yet when you run a report of this year's giving, the system adds in the gifts from her friends only once.

3. Tracking pledges is also important for successful fundraising. Your database should not only track payments and due dates but also make it easy for you to send reminders.

4. Relationships are essential to successful fundraising, so your database should be able to tell you, for example, the friends of your board members and who sat at which table at your fundraising event. Which people, in addition to being donors, are also clients of your nonprofit or have friends or family who are clients?

5. And last but certainly not least, any system should make it easy for you to get information out of it. That includes simple exports of information to use in contacting donors as well as ones to analyze your success by computing, for example, the percent of people solicited who actually made a gift, how many people gave both this year and last year (and how many didn't), which people increased or decreased their gifts over prior years, etc.

Those are the really essential things you need to track, but most CRM systems today come with additional bells and whistles that help you communicate with your constituents and solicit them in different ways. These features might include the following:

1. Easy execution of mail merges will save you hours of extra work. Some systems allow you to create a single letter on the spot as well as export a list of thousands of names for a bulk mailing.

2. Bulk email distribution is a nice addition. You could export your email list to Constant Contact, MailChimp, or a similar service, but why bother when so many CRMs come with that facility built in?

This module should also include templates for creating designed emails using HTML coding and the means to track receipt of and response to your emails.

3. Online donations can make up 50 percent or more of most charities' gifts these days. Your data system should allow you to collect donations online, automatically enter the donations into the database, and send an automated receipt.

4. Special events require tracking of many, many details. You could do that in a spreadsheet, but it is much better to do it from your database so that specific information (such as who asked to be seated next to whom) is right there with everything else you know about your constituents.

5. Mobile access to your database is essential when you're out visiting donors and really helpful at events, where you might need it to process contributions and auction payments.

6. Peer-to-peer fundraising is popular with younger donors, who like to see who else has made a contribution, and it's a great way to expand your donor base. Some CRMs come with this facility fully integrated, recording gifts directly in your database and soft-crediting the people doing the fundraising.

Here's a short and highly opinionated list of fundraising CRM systems you might consider. (**Note:** Prices are based on my experiences with specific lists. Prices will vary depending on the number of constituent records you have and how well you have organized your existing information before moving it into the new system. "Garbage in, garbage out" is all too true in this case, so take the time to clean up and organize your data before turning it over for incorporation into your new CRM software.)

Raiser's Edge is the gold standard in CRMs. It holds tons of information about each constituent, relates the information in ways to help you fundraise, and provides the means to communicate effectively through any channel. It also helps you analyze your data to determine your best prospects, how much to ask for, and more. Mobile access and peer-to-peer fundraising are bonus features. It is, however, expensive. Purchasing the system and setting it up can easily cost you $20,000 or more. It also requires significant training to make the most of it. To be fair, it really is designed for large organizations. Parent company Blackbaud also makes a less expensive CRM called eTapestry with fewer features.

DonorPerfect is my runner-up. It does about 85 percent to 90 percent of what Raiser's Edge does with purchase and setup costs around $5,000 or more. A few clicks are all it takes for all the most important standard fundraising reports. What's more, it is very easy to add fields and modify reports to suit your purposes, whereas with Raiser's Edge, it's more likely you'll have to go back to the software's programmers for paid help. DonorPerfect also provides mobile access and peer-to-peer fundraising. It is easy to learn, and any computer-savvy person can sit down and start working with it in minutes.

DonorView is a newer program that packs in a lot of features and is very easy to learn. What's great is that the upfront costs are $0! That's right: It converts your data and gets you started for nothing. It also has amazingly responsive customer service. Particularly impressive is DonorView's commitment to continually expanding its features, especially in response to users' requests. Keeping track of multiple salutations and pledge tracking is restricted. The reporting facility is limited; you filter your records to include the ones you're interested in and then export them to Excel, where you do the refinements and formatting. (Not a problem if you're a power user in Excel; time-consuming if you're not.) It offers peer-to-peer fundraising, but at the time of this writing (November 2017), it offers minimal mobile access to donor records.

All three programs are cloud-based, making your information available to you from any computer, anywhere. A quick summary appears on the following page.

Raiser's Edge (blackbaud.com)

PLUS: Excellent reporting and tracking

MINUS: Complicated to learn; closed system; expensive to customize

RELATIVE EXPENSE: $$$$

DonorPerfect (donorperfect.com)

PLUS: Intuitive to use; easy to customize; open, easily adaptable system.

MINUS: Custom reports somewhat difficult to create.

RELATIVE EXPENSE: $$

DonorView (donorview.com)

PLUS: No upfront costs; excellent support; can be customized at no cost to a point. Easy to learn.

MINUS: Reporting module not developed; limited mobile access at present

RELATIVE EXPENSE: $

For descriptions and reviews of many other fundraising programs, see capterra.com/fundraising-software.

Chapter 3

Supporting Materials

Anyone considering your request for a donation—whether an individual, a foundation, a corporation, or a government agency—will want evidence that your organization is legitimate and financially sound. Each entity also will want to know all about your programs, including who your clients are, how you carry out your programs, and how you make your services known. Therefore you should have at the ready a number of standard documents, which I have listed in this chapter. Don't be intimidated by the long list: Many of these documents you already have or can create quickly.

Nonprofit Status

Keep handy printed and digital copies of the certification of your nonprofit status from the IRS or state agency. Every institutional funder will want to see this certification. If the IRS has certified you, there is no need to provide evidence of state exemption as well. (**Note:** State nonprofit certification and state sales tax exemption are not the same thing.)

Organizations just starting out and without nonprofit status can sometimes apply for funding through a *fiscal sponsor*—that is, an existing nonprofit (usually a service organization in your field or a community foundation) that allows new organizations to apply for funding through it, using its nonprofit status as the necessary certification. Some will even make it possible for you to raise funds online. Fiscal sponsors usually take a fee of 6 percent to 8 percent of any funds raised for providing this service.

If you are considering using a fiscal sponsor, check out candidates carefully on guidestar.org to judge their financial stability. Stay away from a fiscal sponsor with a history of budget deficits; it might be tempted to use the money designated for a sponsored organization for its own expenses.

If possible, talk to others who have used the fiscal sponsor to see what it's like to work with them. And ask questions directly to the sponsor. Beyond asking about the fees it charges, you will want to ask if the sponsor makes your funds available to you immediately and how it handles donor acknowledgments.

Board List

Funders will want to see a list of the members of your board of directors, usually including their professional affiliations. Additionally, some funders will also want to know the date each person joined your board. This allows the funders to see who and what type of people support your organization, which helps them judge if there is adequate support to make your nonprofit viable and the quality of your leadership. A short bio of the head of your board might also be requested from time to time.

State and/or Federal Financial Reports

Whether you file IRS Form 990, 990-EZ, or 990-N, it will need to be part of most grant applications. State financial returns might also be required. Check the regulations for the agency responsible for nonprofits in your state. If your organization is behind in submitting these reports, get up to date before seeking funding. If you are using a fiscal sponsor, you will be asked to submit that organization's Form 990.

Audited Financial Statements

Foundations and government agencies prefer that nonprofits have an annual audit, which results in an audited financial statement prepared by an accountant outside your organization. Smaller organizations might instead have a much less costly financial review performed. The point of both statements is to assure a funder that an independent financial professional has seen your financial records and has certified that they are accurate.

A financial review is sort of like someone checking over your homework. The auditor certifies that he has examined your records and that all appears to be in order. A financial audit requires the accountant to verify your financial information to a greater degree, including contacting a sample of your donors and vendors. An audited statement also conforms to strict industry guidelines on how you account for income and expenses. Both audits and reviews examine your internal controls and look for any evidence of fraud.

Budgets

A budget provides a funder with a lot of information: (1) It gives a picture of the size of your operation by stating how much you take in and spend in a year. (2) The balance between income and expenses shows if you are being financially responsible by working within your means. (3) Because funders will have seen hundreds if not thousands of budgets over the years, a budget will instantly reveal if you know what you're doing by what line items you have included—and which ones you have left out.

Working budgets can contain dozens of lines of specific expenses. Don't send that to a funder. Condense it into a readily scannable number of lines that highlight major expenses without undue detail. For example, you can have a line called "Occupancy" that includes your rent, utilities, and insurance, reducing three lines to one. Itemize only significant expenses. If your budget is $100,000, for example, a $50 filing fee is not significant. You should also create a budget with similar line items for any project for which you seek funding.

Be careful preparing budgets: Don't over- or underestimate. You will be asked to submit a financial report to funders based on this budget. You can read more on budgets at <u>grantadviser.com/budget</u>.

Staff Information

Short, one-paragraph bios of the most important staff members (and consultants) working on a project help demonstrate the depth of experience your nonprofit possesses. Occasionally a funder will also ask for an organizational chart, showing who reports to whom.

Mission Statement

A mission statement is a straightforward description of (1) what your nonprofit does, (2) how it does it, and (3) the values that underlie what you do. For help with creating a mission statement, see the list of additional resources at the back of this book.

History and Background

It's important to have several versions of your nonprofit's history to suit different requests. Typically, a funder will request short history of a page or less. You might consider rewriting your history to emphasize your experience in a particular area if you are applying for project funding. A history should include the date your nonprofit began operating (including the time it was functioning before actually becoming a nonprofit), who founded it, significant accomplishments, and any special recognition it has received.

Testimonials

It's always good to allow other people to say something nice about your work. Testimonials from clients, civic leaders, or funders add credence to your descriptions of what you have accomplished. It's a good idea to keep a collection of these on hand to use as needed. Don't feel shy about soliciting these. Everyone in the business understands how important they are, and the people you have served will be happy to give something back.

Case Statement

A case statement contains all the important facts about your nonprofit, including its mission statement, important parts of its history and background, a list of accomplishments, descriptions of programs, and methods of funding. It is most frequently used in relation to a specific campaign, especially capital campaigns. It can also be the basis for the leave-behind piece described in Chapter 4.

Video

Increasingly, funders request short videos demonstrating your work. Make sure you think seriously about what you submit. Content is more important than production values. (I once received a $150,000 grant with a rather dark video shot with my iPhone.

Despite the gloom, it clearly showed the teaching process that interested the funder.) That said, don't send something boring, like someone standing behind a podium talking the entire time. Much more interesting would be to send a video of a question and answer period where there is interaction between the speaker and audience. (**Hint:** If you plan to film a lecture or discussion with a Q&A, ask the presenter to repeat questions made by audience members. Too often, these questions are not caught on tape, and chances are that half of the people in the audience couldn't hear the questions either.)

Marketing Materials

Funders will want to know how you are attracting people to your organization and programs. Keep a file of any flyers you print, as well as printed and PDF copies of web pages and emails promoting your organization or program.

Client Demographics

Last but certainly not least, maintain statistics on the people who benefit from your organization's work. Funders will want to know things such as how many people currently benefit and how that number has changed over time, as well as demographic information (age, gender, orientation, ethnicity, and economic status). That information can be gathered up front much more easily than after a program ends, so build questions about demographics into your application or participation forms.

Public Information

In addition to having the preceding information ready to give funders on request, you should also make much of it available publicly, which you can do through your website and/or your guidestar.org profile. These are the first places people interested in your organization will go for information.

GuideStar's database includes any organization with nonprofit status, and it allows nonprofits to upload information about themselves and receive in exchange its Bronze, Silver, Gold, and Platinum designations for transparency. (GuideStar will also accept contributions on your behalf and pass them on to you.) Keep your GuideStar profile current! Nothing creates a bad first impression faster than out-of-date information.

After you have the right people on board and your information organized, it's time to look at what you need to do to prepare to raise money from each of the potential funding sectors. The remaining chapters discuss these sectors one by one.

Chapter 4

Soliciting Individuals

Seventy-two percent of all donations in the United States come from individuals, and when you add bequests, individuals are responsible for a whopping 80 percent of all charitable giving. Individuals will very likely be the principal source of funds for your nonprofit, too. You will want to ask individuals for support both in person and through mail, email, and phone. Each method requires slightly different preparation.

Personal Solicitations

In personal solicitations, the solicitor who asks for the contribution is the critical factor, but preparation is important, too. This includes not only preparing the solicitor to ask for a donation but also doing your homework so that you know as much as possible about the interests and giving habits of the potential donor. Several vendors offer *wealth screening services*, which provide you with information on your prospects likely wealth, the value of their home, and nonprofits they support (and at what level), among other things. Some wealth screening services are tied into specific CRM software (described in Chapter 2), so deciding on the best screening service might be part of the CRM decision. It's never too soon to learn more about your donors.

It's helpful for solicitors to have a cheat sheet enumerating your nonprofit's successes and important program facts. Additionally, you might want a leave-behind—that is, a small brochure that outlines the case for support and gives your contact information. It need not be elaborate but should be well designed and contain all the essential facts someone might want when deciding to support your nonprofit.

Mail and Email Solicitations

Most of your donors will be solicited by mail or email. It's tempting to use only email, but postal mail is far from dead. It's especially effective with donors age 60 or older. And as more and more advertising moves to email, a letter in a mailbox is starting to feel special again.

If you've done a good job putting together your mailing lists and uploaded them into a decent CRM program, you have the ingredients for a successful email or mail campaign. Keep in mind that one size does not fit all—the more you segment your list and focus your letter on the particular interests of different groups of donors, the better you will do. For example, a typical breakdown that I use for year-end mailings segments the list into the following categories:

- Prior donors of $1,000 or more
- Other prior donors
- Members/clients with high giving potential as evidenced in wealth screening research, but no prior gifts
- All other members/clients
- Other donor prospects

Don't spend money creating an elaborate brochure to mail your donors. You don't need it. You *will* need a terrific letter to convince donors of the need for your services and your ability to carry them out.

Note: Raising money by phone is increasingly difficult. Most people screen their calls, and even if they pick up the phone, they are likely to be annoyed that you interrupted a conversation or time with their family members or friends. Raising money by phone can also be quite expensive unless it's done completely by volunteers.

Crowdfunding

An increasingly popular and successful means of raising funds (especially with millennials) is *crowdfunding*, in which a great number of individuals make relatively small donations to fund a project or business. Internet platforms that facilitate crowdfunding include indiegogo.com and *kickstarter*.com.

Before you attempt a crowdfunding campaign, ask yourself if (1) your cause is one that will appeal to a great number of people, (2) you have attractive rewards to offer donors at various levels of giving, and (3) you have the means to produce an engaging short video to introduce your project. The last point is an important one: People aren't on the internet to read a long proposal, but they can be captivated by a short, clever video.

Some groups have raised hundreds of thousands of dollars this way, but a lot of factors contributed to their success, including the three I just mentioned. Carefully read the how-to guides provided by each internet platform before deciding on this means of fundraising.

Peer-to-Peer Fundraising

Remember the beginning of Chapter 1, where I said all fundraising is individual fundraising? Well, the perfect example of this is peer-to-peer fundraising. Like crowdfunding, peer-to-peer fundraising depends on receiving many relatively small donations from a large number of people, although in this case you are mobilizing your current donors to help you raise funds.

To raise money peer-to-peer, you will need CRM software that supports this function and several hundred donors willing to participate in your campaign.

How much can you raise this way? The sky's the limit. With one small nonprofit, I easily raised $23,000 in donations for several years and also used it to sell more than $200,000 in event tickets.

Planned Giving

In the fundraising business, when we talk about "planned giving" we refer to gifts made through someone's will or through a financial tool that relates to their estate planning, such as an annuity with a nonprofit as the beneficiary.

If you're a very new nonprofit with a new donor list, receiving gifts through people's estates might be some years off. Soliciting planned gifts requires much research and, well, planning, but you just never know when someone might want to do something special for you, so it doesn't hurt to be prepared to accept a bequest through a will.

To start a planned giving program, you need to (1) let people know that you are willing to accept gifts through bequests and (2) how to word the bequest. You simply add a planned giving page to your website under your donation information. On that page, put something like the following:

> *[Name of Your Nonprofit] would be honored to receive a gift of cash, securities, real estate, or personal property through your will. To make such a provision, we suggest you include something like the following statement:*
>
> > "I give and bequeath ___% of my estate (or $_____) to [Name and Address of Your Nonprofit]."
>
> *We encourage you to seek legal counsel before designing any will provision.*

It's also good for your board to adopt gift acceptance policies that specify, for example, whether you will sell or hold donated stocks and what kinds of personal property (cars, jewelry, art, real estate, etc.) you will accept. Better to do this before receiving a gift of something that might be problematic for you to use or sell.

That's it. You now have a planned giving program. As time goes by, you'll want to mention the existence of the planned giving program in your newsletters or donor mailings. There are other aspects of planned giving, including trusts and annuities, but these are more often relevant only to large nonprofits with substantial financial resources and staff to administer them.

Chapter 5

Special Events

Good stewardship of your nonprofit should include careful analysis of the likelihood of success for any new fundraising venture. This is particularly true when considering special events, as they frequently require a large outlay of cash before any money is received.

Special events can range from a bake sale to a gala dinner-dance for hundreds of your community's social elites, from a neighborhood walkathon to a telethon broadcast on local radio or television. The scale of your event needs to match your nonprofit's capacity for carrying it out.

A seated dinner with one or more honorees, a live auction, and corporate sponsors will likely be beyond the reach of new or small nonprofits. Even a barbeque and silent auction might require more organizational time and talent than you can muster. Seriously examine if you have the volunteer and staff resources to carry out a particular event.

You will also want to ask yourself if your existing donor base can support the event. Can they afford a high-priced ticket? Might the event attract new donors to your cause? You also want to determine if event ticket sales will be new income or merely shift your loyal annual fund donors to event ticket buyers. The latter will result in a net reduction of fundraising income due to the cost of the event.

There are additional opportunities and challenges unique to raising donations through events you should consider.

Special events must be financially successful. This should be obvious, but in the excitement to have the best band perform and perfect flowers on the tables, expenses can easily get out of hand and eclipse the income from the event. The resulting event shortfall then drags down the nonprofit instead of supporting it.

Create realistic income projections, allowing room to exceed the projection. Assign someone to maintain a tight grip on the expense budget, whether you're paying for cupcake mix or renting the largest ballroom in your town.

Motivating board members and volunteers is one of the major reasons to do a special event. Many board members quake at the thought of asking a friend to give $100 to the annual fund but have no problem asking that same friend to buy a $250 gala ticket. Selling tickets is just easier than asking for donations for many people.

Really successful special events are volunteer (not staff) driven. It's only by bringing in people from your volunteers' and board members' networks that you can reach the critical mass of participation needed to make an event financially successful. If you don't have a dedicated core of volunteers to work on your event, don't do it.

Special events can be the black hole of staff time. Even the most well-intentioned volunteers can overwhelm staff with event details, obsessing over tablecloth colors and revising the seating chart for the millionth time. Don't authorize a special event unless you know that your staff members can add it to their other duties and/or accept the fact that nothing else will get done during the two months leading up to your major event.

Hiring a special events consultant will provide valuable expertise and experience, but the consultant will require staff support that will still eat into time dedicated to other staff responsibilities.

Allow sufficient planning time. A major fundraising dinner with one or more honorees will require advance planning of a year. Six months or more might be needed to gather high-quality items for an auction. Create a realistic timeline specific to your event, and stick with it.

Games of chance might incur government regulations. If you're planning a casino night or even a raffle, check with local and state regulations to make sure you stay on the right side of the law. For example, if you sell raffle tickets for a suggested donation, the buyers can count that as a tax-deductible donation, but if the price of the ticket is not voluntary, it not only isn't tax deductible but might also need to be licensed by your state's gambling authority.

Programming must reflect your nonprofit's mission and values. You want the special event to educate participants about what you do and create positive publicity, so choose your venue, performers, speakers, and honorees carefully. Is the most expensive hotel in town the right venue when you're raising money for the homeless? Should an environmental charity honor a real estate developer with a less than sterling environmental record?

Be clear with honorees about expectations for fundraising. It's common to expect a corporate honoree to make a major contribution to the event. With individuals, it varies. You would likely expect a philanthropist you're honoring to make a major contribution, but if the honoree is a practitioner in your nonprofit's field the person might not have the means to provide major support. In any case, be clear about fundraising expectations and goals.

Special event donors are different than regular donors. Face the fact that most special event donors will give only through special events. Set your expectations accordingly.

Be innovative. Try to think beyond the events that every other charity does. For example, try a "practice-a-thon" for a youth orchestra, where the students ask friends and family to sponsor their practice time for a week. Prizes for the students would be the only expense, resulting in a high net profit.

You can raise a lot of money with special events but do so with your eyes wide open to the difficulties as well as the potential.

Chapter 6

Foundations

Foundations provide approximately 15 percent of philanthropic dollars. The number of foundations has grown rapidly during the last twenty years and giving has nearly doubled since 2003, but the number of nonprofits seeking support has also grown. In addition, many foundations support only preselected organizations known to the founders and trustees. They accept applications only by invitation. That said, if you have some well-connected people on your board, you might be able to finagle an invitation to apply to one of these foundations, so keep reading.

The first step to prepare to raise money from foundations is to put together the supporting materials described in Chapter 3. Most of these will be asked for as part of a grant proposal.

Next, you will need to research which foundations are likely supporters of your nonprofit, and lastly, you'll need a well-written proposal describing the issue your nonprofit seeks to address, your qualifications to address this issue, what you expect to accomplish, and how you will go about reaching your objectives. For these steps, you will need either a professional fundraiser well versed in grant writing or someone willing to learn how to do it.

Hiring a grant writer can be tricky because it's not always easy to evaluate the merits of the writer's work. Going by the writer's success rate can be misleading. As I mentioned in Chapter 1 when discussing consultants, many factors influence the success of any donation, and this is certainly true of foundation grants.

A grant writer who works primarily for large, established organizations will likely have a much better success rate than one working with emerging nonprofits like yours, even if the latter is more experienced and capable. It doesn't mean the first grant writer is better, just that she has more successful clients.

You can, however, evaluate the quality of the writing by requesting a writing sample and ask yourself: On first reading, is the issue being addressed clear to you? Do you understand how the program will be carried out and what it is expected to accomplish? Does jargon obscure any points? Does it make you want to support this nonprofit?

If you do decide to hire a grant writer, remember that professional fundraisers work for set fees, not commissions. Expect to pay between a few hundred to several thousand dollars for a grant writer's work, depending on the complexity of the application and the quality of raw materials you provide the writer.

Grant writing isn't brain surgery or rocket science. It's something that can be learned in a short time, and if the person working on the proposal is already knowledgeable and passionate about your organization, you'll start out a step ahead.

I humbly recommend my book *The Wise Guide to Winning Grants* for those who want to learn to do it themselves. There are literally dozens upon dozens of other books on this subject, and the Foundation Center offers a series of online courses as well as other web resources at grantspace.org.

There can be a three- to six-month or longer turnaround time between applying for a grant and hearing the foundation's decision, so plan far ahead when pursuing foundation grants.

Chapter 7

Corporations

Corporation grants come in many forms and sizes, and several offices within a corporation can make them.

Sponsorships

Corporations give sponsorship support to nonprofits (and to for-profits, including professional sports teams) with the expectation that the company will receive specific recognition in exchange. Marketing departments usually handle sponsorships.

You'll need detailed numbers and demographic information on the audience who will learn about the sponsorship through your organization to help the marketing department justify the expense. Also, the broader your nonprofit's reputation, the more attractive it will be as a sponsorship "property."

In-Kind Support

Donations of products or employees' time and talents to nonprofits are called *in-kind support*. The corporate contributions office, foundation, or marketing department might facilitate these donations. Free advertising through print and radio should not be overlooked.

Many corporations outsource the distribution of free stuff to organizations such as good360.org and techsoup.org. All you will need to access these items is a computer to fill in the request forms and nonprofit status. Local offices of major corporations usually handle donations of volunteer time and expertise.

Grants

Grants are money given to nonprofits to advance their mission or for a specific project. They are usually given by a company's independent foundation, although sometimes the corporate contributions office gives them. Those given by the company foundation are no different than those given by private foundations, although there might be a greater expectation for public recognition.

You'll need the same information for pursuing corporate foundation grants as for private foundation grants, described in Chapter 6. Corporate grant applications will sometimes take on the aspect of a sponsorship request, asking for detailed information on how the grant will be acknowledged and who will be made aware of the award.

An important factor in seeking corporate support is to match the reach of your nonprofit with the reach of the corporation—that is, small, local nonprofits should seek funds primarily from local businesses or local branches of major corporations, whereas large nonprofits can be competitive in seeking funds from major corporations.

For example, if you're a small nonprofit starting out, you probably will not be successful getting a grant from a national bank's foundation, but you might be successful appealing to the manager of its local branch for a small grant to for use in your community. Other local businesses (dry cleaners, grocers, etc.) like to be seen supporting worthy causes in the communities where they do business.

Before investing huge time and effort in corporate fundraising, keep in mind that corporate gifts account for only 5 percent of all philanthropic dollars, and much of that consists of drugs donated by pharmaceutical companies. Also, the biggest recipients of corporate sponsorship are professional sports.

Chapter 8

Government Agencies

Government grants are not for beginners. They are frequently complicated to do and have substantial record-keeping requirements. When trying to decide if you're ready to apply for a government grant, keep these five important things in mind:

1. Government grants are highly competitive.

2. The turnaround time between the application and the awarding of grants can be as much as a year.

3. Many newer and smaller organizations aren't eligible because of requirements that a nonprofit must have been in operation for several years and have a budget of a minimum size.

4. Many government grant applications are lengthy and difficult to complete, requiring a significant investment of time and effort.

5. Many government agencies require that you prequalify as a vendor before submitting a grant application, thus making the process even longer.

Government grants can be broken down into three categories:

1. Formula grants are awarded to nonprofits to carry out a specific predetermined task for the government. Many education, social services, and health grants fall into this category.

2. Project grants pay for work proposed by the nonprofit, just like foundation grants (covered in Chapter 6).

3. Discretionary grants are made because of who you know. Also known as *earmarks* or derisively as *pork*, these grant requests are made directly to a legislator who then attaches your request to a pending bill. Small nonprofits might find success along these lines with city or state officials.

As you can see, a lot of work and planning is involved in applying for government support, but there is also the potential for a substantial award. And after all, who wouldn't like to see some of their tax dollars coming back to support a nonprofit they love? Just be realistic about your potential for success before investing time and money in applying for a government grant.

Glossary

Case statement: A summary of all the important facts about your nonprofit, including its mission statement (see below), accomplishments, programs, and funding.

Constituent Relationship Management systems: Software used to track all aspects of a donor's or client's relationship to an organization, including donations, participation in activities, and their personal and business relationships to the nonprofit's volunteers and leaders and to each other.

Crowdfunding: Raising funds by going directly to the public. Examples include kickstarter.com (for cultural projects), indiegogo.com (for entrepreneurial projects), and gofundme.com (for anything).

Discretionary grant: A grant made at the instigation of an individual based on his/her knowledge of your nonprofit rather than a formal application and a review of the charity's qualifications. These can be found at some foundations and also appear as "earmarks" made by government officials.

Earmarks: Discretionary grants made by government officials, often as part of unrelated legislation. They are derisively referred to as "pork" or "pork barrel" funding.

Fiscal sponsor: A nonprofit that allows new organizations without nonprofit status to apply for funding using its nonprofit status, most often provided by service organizations for a specific sector and occasionally by community foundations.

In-Kind support: Gift of anything other than money, including goods, materials, or someone's time. In-kind gifts are often critical for small nonprofits.

Mission: Why your nonprofit does what it does (feed the hungry, educate children, etc.).

Mission statement: A short description of an organization that is used as a touchstone when creating programs and succinctly describing what you do and why you do it. It is not a tagline, which is a short catchphrase and can be helpful but does not contain as much information as a mission statement.

Peer-to-peer fundraising: Allows you to empower volunteers to fundraise on your nonprofit's behalf. This method is frequently done in a competitive framework, such as raising money through walkathons and other participatory events, although it also can be used for general contributions unrelated to an event. Many fundraising software programs include this capability.

Soft credit: In fundraising, refers to crediting a contribution to more than one person or organization in a way that doesn't double-count the contribution in financial reports. For example, someone donates to your nonprofit at the request of one of your board members. The gift gets credited to the donor and soft credited to your board member, allowing you to track how much the board member has raised as well as how much she has given.

Wealth Screening Service: A service provided by several vendors to identify which of your donors have both the means and the proclivity to make a significant donation to your nonprofit. Means (or capacity) is determined by the value of their home, businesses they own, and gifts they have made. Their proclivity to give to your charity can be assessed by looking at gifts to similar nonprofits combined with the currency and frequency of gifts to your nonprofit.

Additional Resources

Getting Started

Colvin, Gregory L. *Fiscal Sponsorship: 6 Ways to Do It Right*, 2nd ed. San Francisco: Study Center Press, 2006.

BoardSource. (https://boardsource.org) Everything you need to know about boards and their function in a nonprofit, from recruiting board members to understanding financial statements.

Free Management Library: How to Start a Nonprofit.
(https://managementhelp.org/startingorganizations/start-nonprofit.htm) A wealth of information from consultant Carter McNamara.

Mission Statements

GrantSpace. (https://grantspace.org) Includes a basic guide to writing mission statements.

NonProfitHub. (https://nonprofithub.org) Provides a very helpful chart of what makes a good (and a bad) mission statement.

Budgets

Quick, James Aaron, and Cheryl Carter New. *Grant Seeker's Budget Toolkit*. New York: John Wiley & Sons, Inc., 2001.

Thompson, Waddy. *The Who, What, When, Where, and How of Grant Budgets*. (https://grantadviser.com/budget)

Data Management

Capterra. (https://capterra.com) An exhaustive listing of CRM systems.

Idealware. (https://www.idealware.org) Offers a free guide: *A Consumers Guide to Low-Cost Donor Management Systems*. Descriptions of 35 programs and reviews of the 11 best values.

Individual Giving

Burk, Penelope. *Donor-Centered Fundraising*, U.S. ed. Burk & Associates Ltd., 2003. Number one book on motivating individual donors and communicating with them.

Robinson, Ellis M.M. *The Nonprofit Membership Toolkit*. Jossey-Bass, 2003.

Trenbeth, Richard P. *The Membership Mystique*. Taft Group, 1986. Out of print but easy to find used copies. Lacking information on the data and communication advances of the last twenty years, but still an excellent guide to the psychology of membership programs.

"How to Get Your Whole Organization behind Major Gift Fundraising." (https://trust.guidestar.org/how-to-get-your-whole-organization-behind-major-gift-fundraising) Gail Perry in the GuideStar Blog.

"Major Gifts Fundraising: The Questions I Hear Most Often." (https://trust.guidestar.org/blog/major-gifts-fundraising-the-questions-i-hear-most-often) Andy Robinson in the GuideStar Blog. (trust.guidestar.org)

Grant Writing Guides and Research

Heath, Chip, and Dan Heath. *Made to Stick: Why Some Ideas Survive and Others Die*. Random House, 2007. A great guide to writing persuasive copy.

Teitel, Martin. *The Ultimate Insider's Guide to Winning Foundation Grants: A Foundation CEO Reveals the Secrets You Need to Know*. Emerson & Church, 2012.

Thompson, Waddy. *The Quick Wise Guide to Writing Grant Proposals*. Stitch-in-Time Books, 2017.

Thompson, Waddy. *The Wise Guide to Winning Grants*. Stitch-in-Time Books, 2017.

Foundation Directory Online. (https://fconline.foundationcenter.org) The Foundation Center's directory will usually be your first stop when researching the 140,000 U.S. foundations (private or corporate). Also includes government funding.

Foundation Search. (https://foundationsearch.com) Based in Canada, this database contains information on more than 120,000 foundations. The ability to search by grant recipient and the grant details and the summaries provided are particularly useful. For an additional fee, you gain access to a second database with information on corporate and government funding.

GrantAdviser. (https://grantadviser.com) Free resources on the entire grant-seeking process, including working as a freelance grant writer and special resources for fundraising in the arts, from Waddy Thompson.

GrantSpace. (https://grantspace.org) The Foundation Center offers a wide range of helpful information on this website, most of it for free, including courses in various aspects of seeking grants and a library of sample grant proposals.

GrantStation. (https://grantstation.com) A general-purpose online database for those seeking grants in the United States, Canada, and internationally. GrantStation has omitted foundations that do not accept unsolicited proposals and others that offer only scholarships. This results in fewer foundations than in some other databases, but more complete information is given here for most of the foundations that might help you. Information on corporate and government grants is also included. This is a pay service, except for a free weekly newsletter.

GuideStar. (https://guidestar.org) Database of every nonprofit organization in the United States, including foundations, with web links and IRS informational returns that include (for foundations) the grants they have made.

Corporate Fundraising

Martin, Patricia. *Made Possible By: Succeeding with Sponsorship*. Jossey-Bass, 2004.

Skildum-Reid, Kim, and Anne-Marie Grey. *The Sponsorship Seeker's Toolkit*, 4th ed. McGraw-Hill Education, 2014.

International Events Group. (https://sponsorship.com) The authority on corporate sponsorship. Offers excellent one-day seminars on the subject.

About the Author

Waddy Thompson's 35-year career in arts administration encompassed work for a wide variety of organizations serving music, dance, theatre, literature, and visual arts. He has held positions at The Whitney Museum of American Art, InterSchool Orchestras of New York, New York Foundation for the Arts, Poets & Writers, OPERA American, Second Stage Theatre, Symphony Space, and the Authors Guild Foundation. His responsibilities at these organizations have included fundraising, donor-advised funds, marketing, communications, and various administrative areas. He has secured donations, grants, and bequests up to one million dollars from the full spectrum of funding sources.

He is also the author of *The Wise Guide to Winning Grants* (Stitch-in-Time Books, 2017), *The Complete Idiot's Guide to Grant Writing* (Alpha Books, 2011), and numerous articles in *The NonProfit Times* and other periodicals. He has taught grant writing for New York University's Heyman Center for Philanthropy and Fundraising, and he has been a guest speaker and/or workshop presenter for several university programs and various arts councils and conferences.

Mr. Thompson is also a composer and holds degrees from Eastman School of Music (BM) and Florida State University (MM and DM).

Also by Waddy Thompson

The Wise Guide to Winning Grants (Stitch-in-Time Books, February 2017)

The *Quick* Wise Guide to Writing Grant Proposals (Stitch-in-Time Books, November 2017)

You can find more information on fundraising at https://GrantAdviser.com.

www.ingramcontent.com/pod-product-compliance
Lightning Source LLC
Chambersburg PA
CBHW052136010526
44113CB00036B/2280